GW00630782

God's People at Worship

Prayer

*Creative ways of praying
together in all-age worship*

Rowena Webster

*Jointly published by
Division of Education and Youth
and
Methodist Publishing House*

First published May 1994

© Methodist Church Division of Education and Youth

ISBN 0 7192 0194 2
ISBN 1 85852 013 4

Illustrations: Helen Mahood and John Dollery

Jointly published by
Methodist Church Division of Education and Youth
2 Chester House, Pages Lane, London N10 1PR
and
Methodist Publishing House
20 Ivatt Way, Peterborough PE3 7PG

Printed by
Clifford Frost Limited, Lyon Road,
Windsor Avenue, London SW19 2SE.

God's People at Worship

An introduction to the series

'*God's People at Worship*' is a series of booklets about Christian worship, particularly when all ages are involved.

For simplicity, the phrase *all-age worship* is used throughout the series, despite its shortcomings. The word *worship* should need no qualification. In worship, people offer themselves — with all their similarities and differences (including their ages) — to God. Unfortunately, *worship* has come to be seen as a mainly adult activity. To describe it as *all-age* provides an important reminder that it is the business of the whole people of God.

The booklets in the series deal with different aspects of all-age worship. The emphasis is mainly practical, looking at *How?* questions. However, *Why?* questions are also dealt with, particularly in the introductory volume, *One.*

'*God's People at Worship*' is for worship leaders; for those who plan, prepare and co-ordinate worship in local churches; for workers with children and young people; for church musicians; for people who are creative in written or spoken word, dance, drama or visual arts; for stewards, members of worship consultations and Church Councils and all those who make decisions about the church's worship. But, above all, our hope is that these booklets will be read and used by Christian people of all ages who care about worship.

Prayer, the seventh booklet in the series, considers ways of praying with congregations of all ages. It explores 'experiential prayer', which the author describes as 'engaging in prayer with the whole person; senses, body, mind, spirit, emotion, personality'. The book is full of ideas, offering exciting and creative possibilities for all ages praying together.

'God's People at Worship' is produced jointly by the Methodist Publishing House and the Division of Education and Youth, in consultation with representatives of the Division of Ministries and the Worship Commission.

The General Editor of the series is Rev. David Gamble, working with an Advisory Group (Mrs Judy Jarvis, Rev. John Lampard, Mr Brian Sharp and Mr Brian Thornton).

Contents

1 Let us pray . . .

This is not a book about prayer as such, nor a book of prayers. It is a practical guide to praying with congregations of all ages. The book does not claim to be original. It tries to avoid gimmicks. Hopefully the ideas it contains will fire the imagination of anyone who plans and leads all-age worship.

Often, the words 'Let us pray' are an invitation for bodies to slump forward into the 'Non-conformist crouch', heads to drop, hands to be clasped and eyes to be closed tight, as if to block all senses but hearing. Although we are praying *together,* we isolate ourselves from other people and from our surroundings as if we can only pray by cutting ourselves off. Perhaps this is why prayer often seems remote and inaccessible.

This book starts from the conviction that prayer involves all that we are, our bodies and our senses, our surroundings and our fellow worshippers. Chapters 2 and 3 explore ways to engage all the senses in prayer and to enable our bodies to become part of our praying (rather than a distraction). Later chapters consider some of the vast range of materials available to help us develop prayer together in all-age worship in new and creative ways.

Though we often pray using spoken words, we can also use other media and aids. Silence helps people reflect and listen to God. Symbols can touch deep within us. We can express joy, confession, gratitude and pleas for help through movement and posture. Or we can make things together — and both the making and the offering can be praying.

Corporate prayer is not a solo addressed to God by the worship leader, but a rich harmony in which all members of the congregation play their part. It is difficult, but worth the effort, because it provides a profound opportunity to engage and be engaged by God. This is one way of understanding the meaning of prayer — engagement with God. Prayer is being open to God and communicating with him. Brother Lawrence, the seventeenth century down-to-earth mystic, called it 'practising the presence of God'. Clearly this is not limited to time spent in church, and some ideas in this book may help readers in their private prayer life, but the major emphasis here is on praying *together.*

When Christian people gather for worship, we come to celebrate what God has done for us and offer our love in response. Prayer is part of that celebration and response. We express awe and wonder at what God is (**A**doration), recognize our unworthiness before him and say we are sorry (**C**onfession). We respond to all that God does for his creation (**T**hanksgiving) and ask for help, guidance and encouragement for ourselves and for others (**S**upplication). These four elements are sometimes called the **ACTS** of prayer and a well-balanced act of worship will contain them all. Each can be done in creative ways.

This book is about prayer, particularly in the context of all-age worship. Children and young people are rarely referred to explicitly, but it is important to be aware of their gifts and graces. They have much to contribute.

Many of the ideas in this book have been 'field tested' in worship and by a group of local preachers in the Grimsby and Cleethorpes circuit. Thanks are expressed to them and to John Dollery for his drawings.

2 Praying through the senses

As the worshippers enter the church on a late September Sunday morning, their senses of smell and sight tell them instantly that today is special. The pungent scent of ripe plums and chrysanthemums; the eye-catching rows of green apples alternating with oranges and tomatoes along each window-ledge; the skilful arrangement of prize marrow, tinned produce, carrots, onions, beans, dahlias, roses and carefully gleaned stalks of barley, around the Communion rail; mouth-watering bunches of grapes swathing the pulpit — all proclaim that today is Harvest Festival.

Our senses are channels through which God communicates with us. Through them we are aware of our surroundings, our fellow worshippers, and, not least, of ourselves as being alive. This chapter considers the senses in turn, identifying some of the opportunities they offer for prayer.

(In many congregations there are people whose senses, particularly of hearing and sight, are impaired or diminishing. Take care not to embarrass or exclude them.)

Sight

Eyes are amazing. Through them we appreciate colour, shape, texture, pattern, light and dark. Sight enables us to make sense of where we are and what is happening. It is strange then, that we generally close our eyes to pray. This may help us concentrate on what is being said and cut out distractions. In the darkness we may feel closer to God. But so many of the things we pray about enter our minds through what we *see.*

Here are some ways to use people's eyes in prayer:

- Ask people what they saw on the way to church that made them want to say 'Thank you, God, it is good to be alive' (e.g. 'Somebody smiled at me' or 'I passed a newly planted tree') or 'We are sorry to let this happen in your world' (e.g. rubbish, vandalized bus shelter, people sleeping rough).

[handwritten margin note: on our way]

- Invite people to look around the church, noting the familiar faces; the table set for communion or with flowers; banners; textures and colours; shafts of light coming through the windows. Then offer adoration and praise.

[handwritten margin note: around us]

- Have something to look at (a picture, projected slide, posters, banner or candle) to evoke awe, to marvel or wonder at, or to engender concern, sadness or pity. Give people time to really look. Then pray about what they have seen or the emotions it has provoked. Alternatively, provide time for silent prayer or meditation.

[handwritten margin note: a focal point]

- Create a 'worship centre', to set the atmosphere for worship and be a focus for prayer. Possibilities include: nails hammered into a wooden cross or candle surrounded by barbed wire or cross of thorns (Good Friday); folded grave clothes beneath a cross for Easter, etc.

[handwritten margin note: worship centre]

Hearing

Prayer is listening and being still to know that God is God. We need to provide time and space for people to be still and listen.

How do we hear God speaking to us when we pray? It could be that suddenly a thought or feeling strikes us; a word or phrase takes on a whole new meaning; we have an overpowering conviction that we must do something or speak to someone; or perhaps a relaxing feeling that some decision we have made is right.

Of course we can hear God in all sorts of ways, not just when we are formally 'praying', so listening to God can begin by using our ears to make sense of the everyday sounds around us.

- Ask people what they can hear at the moment. Be still and listen. From outside there may be traffic noise, voices, wind or rain. From inside, the ticking of a clock, a cough, a baby's cry, or the gurgle of water pipes. Incorporate these things into a prayer of approach. Alternatively, ask what went through people's minds as they heard these sounds, and base a prayer on what is said.

- Listen to news headlines being read or a conversation as a means of initiating prayer.

- Well chosen music can help us focus our thoughts in prayer or meditation, or the music itself can be the prayer. Many choruses and other pieces of music could be used. Taizé chants are an obvious choice, for use at various points in a service: e.g.

Adoration: *Laudate Dominum*
Confession: *Within our darkest hour*
Thanksgiving: *In the Lord be ever thankful*
Intercessions: *Ubi caritas*, *O Lord hear my prayer*.

- It is good to listen and talk to *each other* as well as to God.

- *Praying in pairs*

  Ask people to discuss in pairs what they have been doing or concerned about this week. Then the pairs say short prayers together.

- *Buzz groups*

  Suggest a specific topic (such as famine, homelessness, war or a local issue) for people to discuss in small groups where they are sitting. After a few minutes, ask these 'buzz groups' for comments and ideas for prayer.

- Where the seating and time available allows, divide the congregation into larger groups and give each a different area of concern (e.g. peace and justice, our local community) to talk about. Each group produces a prayer, or ideas for the leader to weave into a prayer.

A *'prayer workshop'*, where people of all ages explore and develop ways of praying, is an ideal way of listening and sharing ideas and insights together.

John Dollery '92

12

Smell

Certain smells evoke places and events from the past. The smell of paraffin in an old-fashioned hardware shop takes me back forty years to my grandmother's house and happy times spent there. The steamy chlorine of traditional swimming baths is another nostalgic smell, as are bonfire night, newly cut grass and passing a fish and chip shop.

Smell played an important role in worship in the Old Testament. There are references to the people's sweet-smelling sacrifice or offering being pleasing to God.

Burning the sacrifice on the altar was an act of devotion and an experiential prayer. Grain offering and incense were also burned.

Smell is powerful in creating 'atmosphere'. Some churches have a musty 'closed up for the rest of the week' smell. Others have the well cared for smell of recently applied floor and furniture polish. Some Christian traditions continue to use incense in worship. Greek Orthodox churches are sometimes decorated with fragrant greenery and bushy herbs such as basil, thyme, rosemary and lemon. As well as the lovely smells at harvest time, there is the fragrance in a church from flowers after a wedding, funeral or flower festival.

- Use the story of the anointing at Bethany (John 12.1-8) as the basis for a meditation. Distribute pleasant things for people to *smell*, such as bottles of perfume, bars of soap, lavender bags and baskets of pot-pourri. Allow time for people to hear the story and savour the fragrances then give thanks for pleasing aromas and loving acts.

- Scented candles can created a pleasing atmosphere for worship, as can scented polish!

- Ask people about their favourite smells — and thank God for them.

Taste *thoughts of can kick start meditation*

A harvest display of flowers, fruit and vegetables delights the eye and nose and often sets the mouth watering too. How might *taste* be used in prayer?

- Pass around dishes or bowls containing different things to eat (crisps, slices of raw carrot, nuts, raisins, grapes, etc.). As people eat, ask them to think about the great variety of flavour, texture, colour and shape of our food. Pray in adoration and praise to God the creator and provider.

- Thinking about people involved in food growing, manufacturing, retailing and preparation can lead to prayers of intercession or confession, reflecting on the hunger in many parts of the world, greed in others and the 'bitter taste' of exploitation of both land and people in many places.

- Sometimes a particular country will feature in the prayers. On a World Church Sunday, or when a group within the church has studied or visited a country, it might be good to have food from that country.

think babies taste to test, learn & discover, as we must do in our faith

Touch

Every part of our body is sensitive to *touch* but here we concentrate on tactile prayers using the hands. (Gestures and other parts of the body are dealt with in chapter 3.)

- Holding something in the hand can be the starting point for prayers of adoration, confession, thanksgiving, intercession or for silent meditation. For example, give everyone a leaf. Ask them to look at the colour, feel the veins and texture, and picture the tree from which it came. Then think how the church worldwide is like a tree with many branches and covered in leaves, each one symbolic of us, individual Christians or worshippers.

- Holding a seed can lead to prayer on topics such as new life, or growth in faith and discipleship.

- Read Mother Julian's reflection, whilst each person holds a hazelnut:

'He showed me a little thing, the size of a hazelnut, in the palm of my hand, and it was as round as a ball. I looked at it with my mind's eye and I thought, "What can this be?" And answer came, "It is all that is made." I marvelled that it could last, for I thought it might have crumbled to nothing, it was so small. And the answer came to my mind, "It lasts and ever shall, because God loves it." And all things have being through the love of God.

'In this little thing I saw three truths. The first is that God made it. The second is that God loves it. The third is that God looks after it.

'What is he indeed that is maker and lover and keeper? I cannot find words to tell. For until I am one with him I can never have rest nor peace. I can never know it until I am held so close to him that there is nothing between.'

(From *Revelation of Divine Love* by Julian of Norwich.)

- Encourage people to feel, look and marvel at a flower, shell, feather or stone. Ask: *'What does it feel like?'*, *'What colours can you see?'*, *'How was it formed?'*, *'What does it tell us about God?'*.

- Give people a photograph, newspaper, coins, keys, diary or copy of the church notices and ask them to think what the object is for. Prayer can develop in various ways; in silence or with the leader responding to thoughts and comments expressed.

- Holding a small paper dove, the symbol of the Holy Spirit, in the palm of the hand can be an imaginative focus for prayer and meditation. People can write on the dove or 'name in their mind' a person or situation for which they want to pray. Then allow time for silent prayer.

- The hand itself can be a starting place. Invite members of the congregation to examine their own hands carefully and then to look at a neighbour's. Think how hands can be used, for good or ill. Offer praise for the marvellous design and usefulness of hands and confession that we misuse them.

Holy Communion

Holy Communion is a wonderful celebration for all ages and involves most of the senses. There is movement, colour, speech, music, emotion . . . God is there doing something special for us! It is the complete experiential prayer.

With our eyes we look at the bread and wine, watch the minister's symbolic actions, read the liturgy.

We hear the 'word', listen to music,

We say prayers and affirm our beliefs,

We walk, kneel, hold out our hands, touch.

We taste bread and wine, symbols of Christ's life

We respond

We receive

We are fed, physically, emotionally, spiritually,

We have time and space to be silent

We communicate with God.

We share with the rest of the church family.

3 Prayer and body language

We come to worship as separate individuals who are already linked together in a special way. Members of a local congregation are part of the Body of Christ, representing Christ in their local community, and also part of the universal Church. In the New Testament, the metaphor of 'the body' describes, very graphically, the important role that each part plays in enabling the whole to fulfil its mission.

As human beings, 'the crown of God's creation', it goes without saying that our bodies are important to us. This chapter looks at some parts of the body and suggests what role they might play in prayer.

Head

Our *faces* give us identity to the outside world. We can 'read' a lot from a person's face about their physical and emotional state. Facial expressions, particularly those of the leader, have a valuable role in corporate prayer.

- *It is important in all-age worship that everyone, young and old, can feel they belong. There are various ways to encourage this.*

  Ask people to look around, acknowledging one another with a nod and a smile of greeting. Notice that everyone has a different face, hair, shape and personality. Give thanks for each person's uniqueness and for what they bring to worship. Affirm that 'all' become 'one', the body of Christ, a community of faith, ready to discover again God's presence.

A kiss of greeting was part of the culture of Christ's time as it is for many people today. As we share 'The Peace' together, a kiss and a hug can be powerful gestures of prayer.

Members of the congregation could look around at one another, as they hold hands and say the words of The Grace.

* *The complexity of the **brain**; our thinking, our imagination and our ability to be spiritually aware, are wonders of our humanity for which to praise God.*

'Brainstorming' is an effective method for gathering thoughts and ideas for prayer. Suggest a word or phrase, for example 'famine' or 'things I am afraid of'. Write up people's immediate thoughts on a board, flipchart or overhead projector, without comment or elaboration. Integrate these into a prayer of petition and intercession. Brainstorming can be used for other kinds of prayer, too.

Thinking is an important part of praying. Silent prayer and meditation can play a significant part in all-age worship, but need careful and creative preparation (see chapter 5). To 'picture' people and places in our heads is a helpful way to pray.

The dictionary defines a 'brainwave' as 'a sudden idea or inspiration'. Is this one of the ways prayer 'works'? Is God speaking to us in these sudden flashes of insight?

In the head also is the *mouth*, mainly used in worship for talking, particularly by the leader. Take care not to talk too much. God gave us one mouth, but *two* ears! Provide time for people to pray silently or encourage individuals to pray aloud spontaneously as they feel led.

Trunk

This large section of the body contains various organs, many of which can have an important bearing on how we pray and what we pray for.

- Phrases such as 'shouldering a burden' and 'a *shoulder* to cry on'. help us to understand our Christian responsibilities in prayer. We support each other through intercession. Some churches have a 'Prayer and Care' book, in which people write the names of people or situations to pray for during worship.

- We talk of getting to 'the *heart* of the matter', implying the centre or kernel of something, and are familiar with the stylized red heart symbolizing love, followed by a word or phrase.

Love is central to our faith and worship and in our praying we grapple with the complexities and depths of this amazing word.

Hold up a large cut-out heart shape as a 'brainstormer' and ask people to call out some of the things they love (likely replies are: my rabbit, ice cream, my mum, holidays, *EastEnders*, Jesus). Weave these into prayers of adoration and thanksgiving.

'God's love changes everything' can be used as a congregational response in prayers of intercession.

The heart pumps blood around the body and, as it beats, is a valuable indicator that we are alive! Engage the congregation (or active members of it) in some vigorous exercise such as jumping up and down on the spot, or hopping from foot to foot until they can feel their hearts beat faster. They could feel each other's wrist pulses. Give thanks for being alive, for vitality, for energy and the ability to enjoy life God's way.

- For most of the time, if we are in good health, we take for granted the functioning of our *lungs*. We breathe without thinking.

  'God is closer to us than the very breath we breathe.'

  'Breath' and *'spirit'* are the same Hebrew word, *ruach*. A common prayer of invocation is *'God is here, His spirit is with us'*. Whether the prayer be said or sung, it is good to follow it with a short period of silence.

  Ask people to be still and become aware of their breathing. Then ask them to say *'God is here'* and breathe in, pause briefly, then breathe out and say *'His spirit is with us'*. Repeat the prayer in this way and then be still, *'resting in the presence of God'*.

  Members of the congregation can blow into their hands, feeling the force of the 'air' coming from their lungs. Inflate balloons or blow bubbles, in order to experience the power of breath/wind. Give thanks for the intricacies of our bodies, for breathing and oxygen, the providence of God in creating and sustaining us and all other parts of His creation. Prayers of confession could be developed about the misuse and abuse of our bodies, the pollution of the land, sea and air, depletion of the ozone layer, greenhouse effect, etc.

  At Pentecost these activities could be used in prayers celebrating the gift of the Holy Spirit. Include a mime or dance involving flame coloured paper streamers.

- We sometimes speak of having a *'gut'* feeling about something. Looking at pictures from newspapers and magazines, or hearing something that provokes a 'gut' reaction is a possible starting point for prayer.

- *'Midriff theology'* is the phrase coined to describe the process, pioneered in certain Latin American Basic Christian communities, by which they study the Bible and respond to it.

  Those involved express their 'gut feelings' at hearing a Bible-related story and then the actual passage of scripture. The reaction, after discussion, then leads to group action. This could provide a good pattern to follow.

Limbs

Here we consider arms and legs, hands and feet and the role of gestures in praying.

- 'The everlasting arms of God' is a comforting 'picture' often used in prayer. *Arms* and *hands* are used in all sorts of gestures, many of which contribute to praying. For instance, 'hugging' conveys comfort and affirmation and is one of the prayerful gestures associated with sharing The Peace. The value of hugging is well developed in the *Little Book of Hugs* and *The Second Little Book of Hugs* by Kathleen Keating. There are insights here for our corporate prayers.

  Other prayerful gestures involving the arms and hands include; standing with the arms stretched upwards; standing, sitting or kneeling with the palms turned upwards in a posture of receiving; making the sign of the cross; 'laying on hands' for blessing or healing; clapping; and of course putting 'hands together' to pray. How people use their hands when praying together is usually a matter of personal choice but sometimes everyone could be invited to do the same thing (for instance, to hold hands for The Benediction).

  Use the arms and hands to mime the Lord's Prayer. There is an excellent version in Maggie Durran's *All Age Worship*. A group could prepare this and teach it to the congregation.

  Invite members of the congregation to draw round their hand and write on the drawing subjects for prayer.

  Think of phrases using the word 'hand', such as 'lend a hand', 'being a person's right hand' and 'hand in hand'. Develop prayers of intercession from these.

John Dollery '9?

- The expression 'on our *knees'* implies being exhausted or overwhelmed with the weight of responsibilities. People in such situations are obviously in need of prayer. The phrase also refers to the traditional posture for praying, which symbolizes humility before God, obedience, submission and dedication.

- We sometimes speak of 'giving prayers *legs'*, meaning to go and do something about the person or situation for which we have prayed. 'Prayer and Care' books often result in practical help for those named. Such actions are not just the extension of our praying but prayer itself. Members of the congregation of any age could prepare greeting cards, bake buns or grow bulbs, etc., to take to ill, sad or housebound people.

- Finally, to our *feet.*

  Ask people to look down at their footwear and then at the shoes of people nearby. What does our footwear say about us? Are we shod for comfort, smartness or the weather? Where have our feet taken us today? For a prayer of approach, encourage people to pray silently for the people and places they encountered on their journey to church. Some members of the congregation may be frustrated because their feet will not 'go' as they would like. They may be in pain. Pray for those who lack mobility.

  As a prayer of response to *'The Word'*, are there places where our feet should take us, people we should visit?

  Make a pilgrimage of prayer around the church, following a trail of paper footprints. (Members of the congregation would enjoy making them by drawing around their feet,

painting them, cutting them out, etc.) The trail could be used like the Stations of the Cross, with the whole congregation moving from one point to another or people can be divided into smaller groups. The 'pilgrimage' could visit the font, communion table, pulpit, organ, cradle roll or 'First Steps' roll, special memorials to local 'saints' and anything else of significance in the local church. At each stopping point on the 'pilgrimage', allow time for silence or spoken prayers prepared by different people. The hymn *'God is here! As we his people'* (HP 653) might help in the preparation of this.

4 Visual aids to prayer

Having something to look at can be a great aid to prayer. There is material all around us which can be used by anyone willing to spend time in preparation, either on their own or with the help of a group.

Begin by thinking through what sort of material will make the particular contribution you want. Where will you get it? How much will you need? How will it be used? Are you going to have one object for everyone to focus on? If so, will it be big enough for everyone to see? Does it stay in place throughout the service or, if not, can it be introduced with the minimum of fuss?

It may be better for the congregation to gather in groups, each having their own object or picture. Will this need complicated instructions, which take time to give and can distract from worship? How easily can people move into groups? What about the less mobile members of the congregation?

Alternatively, everyone could have their own object. If so, how many will you need? How can they be distributed without major disruption? Can people keep them to take away as a tangible reminder of the service?

Newspapers

Newspapers, colour supplements, magazines and catalogues provide a rich resource of pictures and captions on contemporary issues.

- Prayers of confession could be prompted by cutting out photographs of violence, poverty, dereliction, pollution, or scenes illustrating greed, envy or anger. Similar pictures help our intercessions, including photographs of individuals for whom we want to pray. Cuttings can be mounted to form posters or collages before the service by a house group or during the service by part of the Junior Church or a mixed age group.

- Each member of the congregation could bring a picture or cutting that has particularly caught their eye during the week and offer it in worship, either by exchanging with a neighbour (have some spares for those who did not know or forget) or by sticking it on to a visual display board.

- Local newspapers can make prayers more specific. Not only can issues of local concern be shared, but they can awaken our awareness of the needs of people in the community whom we do not know personally. For example, when praying for the bereaved, names cut from the obituary columns could be given to members of the congregation to include either silently or aloud. The births column could feature in prayers of thanksgiving.

- Denominational newspapers and magazines can also provide subjects for prayer.

Graffiti Boards

- Pin a large sheet of paper to the vestibule wall, or any other convenient surface, for people to write up names and situations for which to pray. Graffiti boards serve a similar purpose to 'Prayer and Care' books, but have the added advantage of allowing people to express themselves in drawing, verse and prose rather than simply by entering names. As part of the prayers the sheet of paper can be placed on the communion table.

Stones

Reference has already been made to feeling pebbles and stones. It helps if they are of various types, sizes and shapes. In many parts of the country there are plenty in gardens or by the road side, but the best source may be a beach or a stream bed.

- In addition to holding a stone, members of the congregation can offer their stones as an act of commitment, and the worship leader, helpers or the whole congregation could build a cairn.

  Cairns are sited at significant points along a mountain track. A larger one marks the summit. They grow as a succession of walkers add their own stone to the pile. (So, with disciples on the Christian Journey, each worshipper is a 'living stone' being used in the building of a spiritual temple — 1 Peter 2.5). As the cairn is being constructed, reflect on how each individual stone represents a worshipper. Together, they build 'the body of Christ' in that place.

Lights

When it is dark outside, lights can be used to great effect.

- They can be put out to illustrate the world or individual lives needing the light of Christ and then put on to symbolize our response. This can be particularly appropriate in Advent and Holy Week. Experiment beforehand to discover the minimum of light needed for safety and in order to read.

Candles

There are many imaginative ways of using candles in prayer.

- As someone lights a candle they name a person or situation for meditation and prayer. The congregation focuses on the candle and reflects in silence.

- Worshippers come to a central candle representing Christ, the Light of the World and light their own candle from it as an act of dedication.

- The light can be shared as the light of the Jesus candle is brought to the congregation by one member — a child perhaps, and each lights their neighbour's candle. (Take care not to place the very young or elderly in danger. Avoid dried flower arrangements nearby!)

- Candles or night lights can be used to create shapes such as a cross or Trinity symbol. Those who wish can bring their light to add to the shape.

- Candles can be placed on locations on a world map as a sign of our intercessions for that place.

- Individuals can place candles next to objects symbolizing specific aspects of the community's life, e.g., a bandage for healing, a ring on a cushion for marriage and relationships, a hammer for employment, a spoon for work in the home, a book for education, or a ball for recreation.

Slides

Slides can provide a focus for different aspects of prayer and have great impact. Members of the congregation could bring their own slides, or a sequence can be put together before the service. Given sufficient time, many effective meditations can be prepared using slides to illustrate biblical themes or passages. A live or taped musical accompaniment could also enhance this means of praying.

Rubbish

Things we throw away (bags, packets, cardboard boxes, wrappers, tins, etc.) can be used to create a focus for reflection.

- Such material can be glued on to a sheet to form a cross. Inserted into a three-dimensional cross formed from chicken or plastic garden 'wire', it gives new depth to the idea of recycling — and becomes a powerful experiential prayer. It can be a symbolic act of confession, or a prayer of commitment and dedication on the part of those who put the rubbish into the cross. (After the service the rubbish is disposed of in environmentally friendly ways.)

5 The sound of silence

People often criticize public worship, other than in the Quaker tradition, for not allowing enough time for silent prayer, or enough 'space between words' to let what is said register and become one's own thoughts and prayers.

People need time to really feel that they are in God's presence, that He's there, and to feel comfortable and relaxed enough in body and mind to concentrate on worship and offer the best of themselves. (Arriving early for the service is not always the answer and in many all-age acts of worship it is not possible to have a time of preparation, either 'directed' or quiet.)

It can be strengthening, encouraging and a means of spiritual nurture to pray your own prayers in silence, alongside others in an atmosphere and context of worship.

All the categories of prayer (adoration, praise, confession, thanksgiving, petition, intercession, affirmation, dedication, etc.) can have times for people to add their own silent prayers to what is offered on behalf of all.

Everybody is different and a person's needs differ from one week to the next. Those preparing and leading the prayers cannot accommodate everyone's needs all the time. A time of silence during the confession provides opportunity for people to say 'sorry' for things they might not care to mention out loud. During silence, an individual who feels really angry, bitter or confused might grumble at God, whilst those who are really thrilled about something can also

express their feelings. There needs to be space, too, for personal intercession.

At Holy Communion there is usually plenty of opportunity for silent prayer. It can be helpful to suggest ways to use this time. People might think about the coming week at home, school and work and where they will particularly need God's strength and help; or about the people they can see in church from where they are sitting, or those mentioned in the intercessions.

A period of silence can help after a Bible reading, sermon or hymn, where people have something definite to think about. Or you could provide a focus such as a candle, picture, object to hold, verse of scripture or a line of a hymn and then leave the silence 'undirected' any further.

Alternatively, the leader can guide people's thoughts, in a 'meditation'. Sometimes a significant proportion of the service could centre on a theme with readings, a piece of music, something to look at, something to do, something to say together — all linked together with periods of silence between.

A meditation on 'Living Stones'

Whilst everyone is receiving a stone or small piece of rock to hold, listen to some fairly vigorous music such as *'Jupiter'* from *'The Planets Suite'*. Lower the sound and ask everyone to examine their stone carefully, thinking about how it was formed, the processes that have changed it, its age, strength, etc.

Link with God, creation, *'Rock of Ages'*.

Someone read Isaiah 51.1 *'The rock from which we were hewn'*.

People think about their background, giving thanks for those who care for them, or were a formative influence in their Christian life.

Build a cairn (see page 28) as 1 Peter 2.6-10 is read, or project or display a picture such as the one illustrated or have individual copies for everyone to use and then take home. Sing a suitable hymn such as 'Everybody's building' from *Come and Praise.*

A meditation on Peace and Reconciliation

Collect recent news items and pictures of situations of war, hostility, or misunderstanding. Pass these around the congregation or do a 'brainstorm' exercise about fighting, hatred, anger, etc.

After a period of silence, sing or say *'The Pollen of Peace'* (Corrymeela Community).

Distribute small cut-out paper doves. People hold them in their hands for a while in silence after the reader has reminded them of the power of the Holy Spirit, and the freedom of movement of the dove, to move, change things, etc. (See page 16.)

Then people write on one side of the dove a place or situation they want to pray for where peace or reconciliation is needed. On the reverse they name some person or event in their own lives that they feel 'a need to be at peace' with. After a time of quiet, say a suitable prayer together and share The Peace.

A meditation using modelling clay

Give everyone a small amount of modelling clay or 'playdoh'. 'Brainstorm' on names, titles and characteristics of God. Ask people to use the clay to represent one or more of these.

(If people are hesitant and unsure what to make, a smooth round orb could symbolize the creator . . ., or a hollow ring the perfect, unchangeable nature of God. Three small balls in a triangle for the Trinity, a heart, etc.)

As people fashion their shape, play some quiet music.

Someone then reads Jeremiah 18.1-6 — At the Potter's House.

Allow time for reflection, then all sing or say 'Spirit of the living God' (HP 295) a couple of times, still holding the clay.

6 Responsive prayers

All prayer is a response to God, but the term 'responsive prayer' is generally used to describe prayer in which the congregation is assigned a specific form of response. As well as saying 'Amen' at the end of most prayers, many congregations are accustomed to responding *'Hear our prayer'* to the versicle *'Lord, in your mercy . . .'* Other familiar versicles and responses include:

'God is here'	*'His Spirit is with us'*
'Lord hear us'	*'Lord graciously hear us'*
'Lord have mercy'	*'Christ have mercy'*
'The Lord hears our prayer'	*'Thanks be to God'.*

Many prayers in books include responses. Alternatively, you can devise your own. Keep them short. About half a dozen words is the maximum people can remember comfortably. The versicle needs to be clearly recognizable. Both versicle and response need to make sense on their own. Responsive prayers are easier when the words are set out in a book or worship sheet or when an overhead projector is used.

Responses can be sung. The Taizé chant *'O Lord hear my prayer, . . . when I call answer me'* is popular, as are such Iona Community responses as: *'Kindle a flame to lighten the dark and take all fear away'* and *'Lord, draw near . . . and stay'*. There are many settings for the traditional *'Kyrie eleison'* (Lord have mercy).

Congregations can develop their own sung responses, with accompaniment on instruments such as shakers and chime bars, as well as recorders and other conventional instruments.

The *Lord's Prayer* is said or sung at virtually every service and there is a danger of over familiarity. Occasionally it could be sung to a different tune, such as the 'Caribbean' version. Alternatively, there could be pauses between the phrases to allow people to think about the words. A group might bring to the service something for the congregation to hear or see that has come out of a period of study of this great prayer.

The Lord's Prayer can be said antiphonally, by two sections of the congregations in turn:

Our Father	*Who art in heaven*
Hallowed be thy name	*Thy kingdom come*
Thy will be done	*On earth as it is in heaven*
Give us this day	*Our daily bread*
And forgive us our trespasses	*As we forgive those who trespass against us*
And lead us not into temptation	*But deliver us from evil*
For thine is the Kingdom	*The power and the glory*

For ever and ever

Amen

Rap

In recent years 'rap' has gripped the imagination of the young. In Black and Latin American youth slang, 'rap' means 'to chat' or 'to talk'. As an art form, it refers to a popular type of socially aware improvised 'street poetry'. It is spoken, rather than sung, to a heavy, strong, rhythmic beat. Many young people are adept at writing and performing raps, which can be adapted to any prayer theme. Older members of the congregation may be surprised how stimulating it can be to join in a prayer in this style. Rap lends itself to prayers of joy and celebration and also to serious thought on current issues. It needs to be audible and clear. A leader sets the pace and rhythm and encourages participation. *'Let inhibition go and the prayer will flow'* is the maxim here! The following is part of a rap prayer written by two teenage sisters for a Junior Church anniversary, a traditional subject in a modern style.

Nicola and Carla's 'Anniversary Rap'

Nicola Jiffling kids on a rickety stage
All   It's anniversary, thanks to God.
Carla   Nice warm weather, hot and sunny
All   It's anniversary, thanks to God.
Nicola Girls look smart in brand new dresses
All   It's anniversary, thanks to God.
Carla   Reading, singing, teachers prompting
All   It's anniversary, thanks to God.
Nicola Children reciting, audience clapping
All   It's anniversary, thanks to God.

('Jiffling' is the local word for fidgeting)

Action Prayers

In several of the suggestions in this book — for example, cairn-building, or placing lighted candles on a world map — the action is the prayful response. The action should be proceeded by a time of reflection.

- Prayers of confession could consist of silence for individual thought at the end of which people write (or draw) on a piece of paper specific things for which they need forgiveness. The papers are gathered together (unread) and taken to the worship leader who burns them (on a large metal tray or in a barbecue) and says words assuring the congregation of God's forgiveness.

- At a service in Advent, give people two pieces of paper or thin card cut into the shape of a bauble, with a slit so that they fit together (see illustration, page 41). Invite people to 'write' with their finger things that need 'repentance' in their own life or in society, on two faces of the bauble. On the others they write one or two things that they are hoping will change. They then hang the baubles on the bare Christmas tree.

- For intercessions, create a paper prayer chain. Give each person three strips of gummed paper (the sort used in making Christmas decorations). On the first they write the name of someone they want to pray for, on the second a situation or issue that concerns them and on the third a prayer for themselves. They join the first two strips together and then use the third to link theirs on to their neighbour's chain. All the links are joined into one complete chain which is then placed on or around the communion table in offering to God.

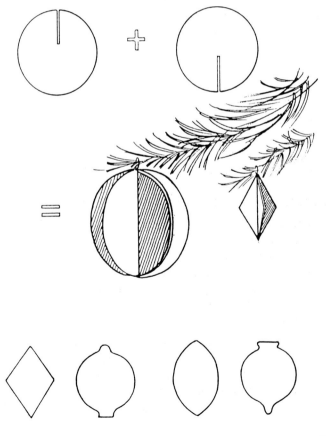

7   Using other people's prayers

Some churches favour prayer book liturgies. Others value extempore prayer, which can bring a sense of immediacy and spontaneity to worship. However, extempore prayer may ramble unless there is a structure to help 'the congregation to accompany the preacher to the throne of grace'! Clarity is always important, but particularly so in all-age worship. It helps to plan the prayers and jot down headings.

An alternative is to use written prayers, either from a book or prepared by a group or individual.

Language is of prime importance. Words need choosing with care, sentences should be reasonably short, and complex structures avoided. In their early years, up to say ten, children think in concrete, literal terms. They can find abstract concepts such as 'eternal', 'holy' or 'worthy' difficult. At the same time it is a mistake to 'talk down' to any group in the congregation. Prayer is more than a succession of words to be understood. Words and phrases can carry an aura creating a captivating atmosphere of wonder and mystery. Make sure that language is inclusive of both sexes and all ages.

Books of prayers

Many books of prayers are available, some designed for use with particular age groups. Worship and learning material such as *Partners in Learning* contains suggested prayers for each Sunday. Reading such prayers can help us in writing our own.

In addition to modern prayers, there are anthologies of great prayers from the past, which have stood the test of time, and which by their very repetition down the centuries, have become part of our heritage. By praying them we link ourselves to this heritage and receive more than the words themselves.

Service books

Many churches use service books from which prayers can be read. If prayers become familiar they bring an added dimension to our corporate praying. However, some prayers in service books are difficult to understand or use old-fashioned or non-inclusive language. It may be possible to adapt these to make them more appropriate for use in all-age worship.

Hymn books

Hymn books have also always been prayer books. Many hymns can be used as prayers (Here, the numbers are from *Hymns and Psalms*, but the hymns are in many books):

134 *'Forgive our sins as we forgive'*. A prayer of confession.

186 *'After darkness, light'*. A marvellous Easter prayer that lends itself to illustration with slides and music as the basis of a meditation on the evening of Easter Day.

250 *'Alleluia, Alleluia, give thanks'*. A joyful prayer of praise that could involve the whole body. It cries out for movement, either by everyone or by a group who have prepared a dance or mime beforehand.

280 *'Breathe on me, Breath of God'*. A prayer invoking the Holy Spirit (see chapter 3, on *lungs*).

290 *'Into a world of dark'*. A prayer workshop would find a lot of scope for visual illustration in this meditative poem.

295 *'Spirit of the living God'*. A popular hymn to sing 'prayerfully'. Follow it with a period of silence.

342 *'For the fruits of his creation'*. Suitable for responsive praying, particularly at harvest.

413 *'We pray for peace'*. This could be spoken either by everyone together or just one voice at a time.

414 *'What does the Lord require'*. The first part of the verse can be said by one voice and the rest of the congregation responds with the last three lines.

503 *'O praise him, O praise him'*. This version of 'The Song of Caedmon' is a prayer of adoration that gives great scope for an art and music workshop.

525 *'Kum ba ya, my Lord'*. Sing the first verse of this prayer of invocation as the response to bidding prayers. Alternatively, invite people to suggest new verses.

530 *'Jesus, stand among us'*. A prayer of invocation, often sung as an introit.

540 *'Open, Lord, my inward ear'*. Read the first two verses together in preparation for a time of silent prayer.

557 *'Prayer is the soul's sincere desire'*. James Montgomery's poetic definition of prayer is an excellent basis for a guided meditation on prayer.

561 *'Father, we thank you'*. The verses of this thanksgiving hymn divide into two parts for antiphonal praying.

572 *'Think of a world'*. As a prayer of thanksgiving this divides well into two parts, either for two sets of voices or for a leader and congregational response.

671 *'Day by day, dear Lord'*. Either said or sung, this is a superb petitionary prayer.

694 *'God be in my head'*. A prayer of invocation.

739 'May the mind of Christ my Saviour'. A good prayer for commitment to discipleship.

776 'Make me a channel of your peace'. This hymn is based on a traditional prayer of commitment.

The Bible

The Bible is a rich source of material for prayer in worship. Some parts are prayers as they stand. There are doxologies, declarations of forgiveness and benedictions. Many passages can be used for meditation either simply by being read or by being made into a banner or collage.

Some psalms lend themselves to use in all-age worship.

Ps 4 (HP835). An evening prayer asking of God's help.

Ps 23 (HP842) The Shepherd Psalm: so familiar yet one to spend some time really 'seeing' and 'feeling' afresh.

Ps 24 (HP843) This prayer of adoration and praise is good for choral speaking.

Ps 51 (HP852) A prayer of confession.

Ps 104 (HP870) Ideal material for a prayer workshop on harvest.

Ps 139 (HP883) A meditative prayer on God's presence and knowledge of us.

Ps 92. Another that could be made into a responsive prayer.

The Magnificat (HP826), Benedictus (HP825) and Nunc Dimittis (HP828) are biblical prayers with an established place in worship, as is Aaron's blessing, Numbers 6.24-26. A concordance can point to many other Old Testament prayers which can be used or adapted for all-age worship (e.g. the prayers of Hannah, Solomon, Ezra and Job, or the 'Servant Songs' of Deutero-Isaiah).

In the New Testament, the Prayers of Jesus are worth exploring (e.g. the Lord's Prayer, Luke 11.2-4; 'Come to me all you who are tired', Matthew 11.28-30; Jesus prays in Gethsemane, Matthew 26.36-46; Jesus prays at the raising of Lazarus, John 11.41-42; Jesus prays when facing death,

John 12.27-28; Jesus prays for his followers, John 17. Jesus prays from the cross, Matthew 27.46; Mark 15.34; Luke 23.34, 46).

The New Testament also contains very usable doxologies and benedictions:

Romans 15.25-27; Ephesians 3.20-21; 1 Thessalonians 3.11-13; 1 Peter 5.10-11; Jude 24-25.

8 ... Amen

This book started from the premise that prayer is important and should involve the whole person. Prayer is also difficult, not least when it is being done together. When all ages are present in a congregation, the challenge is greater still. But it is a challenge well worth taking up!

Hopefully this book has provided ideas and opened up some new possibilities for groups and individuals as they plan and prepare for prayer in all-age worship.

9 Resources for prayer

God's People at Worship
MDEY/MPH
One
David Gamble
Place
Judy Jarvis
People
John Lampard
Rural
Peter Robinson
Story
Michael Townsend
Drama
Michael Austin

Partners in Learning
MDEY/National Christian Education Council

Worship & Preaching
Methodist Publishing House

Companion to the Lectionary
Vols 3 and 4, Epworth Press (see also companion to the
new lectionary, published 1994)

All Year Round
Council of Churches in Britain and Ireland

The Iona Community Worship,
A Wee Worship Book
Wild Goose Publications, 840 Govan Road, Glasgow

Celebrating Together
Prayers, liturgies and songs from Corrymeela, Corrymeela Press

With All God's People — New ecumenical prayer cycle
Vols 1 and 2, WCC

Taizé Chants — Music from Taizé
Vols 1 and 2, Harper Collins

Enfolded in Love — Daily readings with Julian of Norwich
Darton, Longman & Todd

When you pray with 3-6s
When you pray with 7-10s
When you pray with young people
NCEC

Celebrating Christmas Bk1 and 2
Celebrating Harvest
Celebrating Special Sundays
Celebrating Lent and Easter
NCEC

Together (magazine)
National Society

Together for Christmas
Together for Easter
Together for Harvest
Church House Publishing

Help, there's a child in my Church
Peter Graystone, Scripture Union

All Age Worship
Maggie Durran, Angel Press

Children at Holy Communion
  Guidelines
  One Body With Him
  Keeping the Feast
MDEY

Peter and Paula at a Communion Service
Chester House Publications

The Sunday Service Illustrated
MDEY

Instant Art for Church Magazines
Bks 1 and 3, Palm Tree Press

Banners in His Name
Christian Banners, Patricia Nunnerly

Christian Aid Catalogue — including material for all age worship
Christian Aid

Prayer Handbook
Methodist Publishing House

URC Prayer Handbook
United Reformed Church

It's more than shutting your eyes
John S. Lampard, Methodist Church Division of Ministries